To the Herb Lover

Happily, the old saying, "You can recognize a master chef by the seasonings," no longer applies only to the professionals in famous gourmet restaurants, but also to the unknown cooks at home. Gone are the days when every meal was coated with a single sauce—creativity with seasonings is now the norm. Cooking is fun again, and eating has become a pleasure. In addition, food seasoned with herbs is more wholesome. Today, thyme and rosemary, basil, oregano, lemon balm, and mint are as commonplace in any kitchen as pepper and salt. Increasingly, people these days are rarely reaching for the commercial product. The herbs used to improve food must be fresh and home-grown. If they have no garden in which to grow their own kitchen herbs, they can keep a selection of them in flower boxes or pots on the balcony or on the kitchen windowsill.

In *Barron's Herbs* you will find a selection of the most popular cooking herbs that you can plant in your garden or in boxes or pots so that you will be able to grow and harvest fresh herbs all year. The 40 color photographs show you how the plants look. The short, concise notes describe the plants and give useful information about culture, care, harvest, use, and storage. A general section following the notes (beginning on page 43) explains in detail information on planting, care, and harvest in the garden as well as in boxes or pots. Here you will also find tips for storing. Beginning on page 55, you will find a small selection of classic herb recipes for the kitchen.

Barron's Herbs is also a great help in identifying herbs when you are buying them at the garden center or in the market. Now you can easily grow your own herbs yourself.

C0-CFI-017

Photograph on front cover: Basil, back cover: Herb garden.

How to Use This Book

Barron's Herbs presents the most familiar and most popular kitchen herbs. They are arranged according to the length of their life in the garden (annual, biennial, perennial). The order within the three groups is alphabetical. Colored photographs show the characteristics that are important for identifying each plant. Easy-to-understand, concise text descriptions inform the reader about appearance, culture, use, harvesting, and storage. The general section (from page 43) contains a short history of herbs, a selection of classic herb recipes, and additional details about planting, harvesting, and care.

Meaning of the Color Code

To show at a glance what type of location is most suitable for the plant under discussion, the pictures have a color code mark.

　　　　　Sun　　　　　　　　　　　　　Shade

　　　　　Semishade

Explanation of the Descriptive Text

The English plant name commonly used in horticulture appears over each picture. The other common names are given at the beginning of the short text, followed by the Latin name. **Appearance** contains the description of the most important characteristics of the plant, as well as a designation of the plant as an annual, biennial, or perennial. After **Taste,** the appropriate **Uses** are explained. Tips for planting and care are listed under the heading **Garden Culture** or **Pot Culture. Harvest** indicates the best time (season) for picking. The different possibilities for **Storage** of herbs are then discussed.

The Author

Christine Recht writes for various garden magazines and is the author of several gardening books. She draws on her work as well as on practical experience in her own garden.

Pimpinella anisum

Appearance: Up to 19½ in (50 cm) tall, pinnate, bright green leaves, white flower umbels, white seeds in small egg-shaped fruits. Annual.

Taste: Strong spicy-sweet.

Use: Seeds for baking, sweet foods, fruit salad, mushrooms, liqueur.

Garden Culture: At the end of March in the cold frame; beginning of April outside in a sunny area. Cover seeds well; need darkness to sprout. Germination up to 4 weeks. Thin to stand 6 in (15 cm) apart; soil somewhat alkaline. Seeds will not ripen in cool summer.

Harvest: Cut off umbels from time to time when the fruits become brownish. Hang dried bouquets over a clean cloth; shake out seeds.

Storage: In screw-top jars, tin boxes.

Basil

Ocimum basilicum

Appearance: Up to 19½ in (50 cm) tall, squarish stems with bright green, in some varieties red, leaves that arch upward. Small white to pink flowers. Annual.

Taste: Peppery-sweet, very individual, not to be confused with any other herb.

Use: Leaves for tomatoes, sauces, salads, Mediterranean vegetables, fish.

Garden Culture: Sow at end of May in a very sunny spot; will not germinate when night temperatures are under 50°F (10°C). Plants are better than seeds.

Pot Culture: Sow in flats; plant in flowerpot. Grows in pot better than in garden. No fertilizer. Keep damp.

Harvest: Young leaves constantly.

Storage: In vinegar or oil.

Borago officinalis

Appearance: Up to 39 in (1 m) high, bushy plant with hairy green leaves and lustrous gray-blue flowers. Annual.

Taste: Slightly tart, something like cucumber.

Use: In fresh salads, egg dishes, cheese, cottage cheese. Do not cook; use fresh.

Garden Culture: Sow outdoors in April in a sunny spot; damp, fertile soil. Needs much space and much water. Thin to 15½ in (40 cm) apart. Will continue to self-seed.

Pot Culture: Sow in a very large pot; place in a sunny window, or, preferably, on a balcony.

Harvest: Fresh constantly; the youngest leaves are the best.

Chervil

Salad chervil
Anthriscus cerefolium

Appearance: Hollow stems, 23 in (60 cm) high, with soft, bright green leaflets. White flower umbels from May on. Annual.

Taste: Spicy-sweet, anise-like, but milder.

Use: Young leaves before blooming in soups, sauces, salads, omelettes (fines herbes).

Garden Culture: Sow at end of March, 1 row every 3 weeks, in a semishaded spot.

Then you can harvest after 8 weeks and continually thereafter. Smooth-leaved and curly chervil both the same.

Pot Culture: In flats or dishes. After harvest replenish the soil. Do not allow the soil to dry out.

Harvest: Leaflets before flowering.

Capsicum annuum

Appearance: Small, vigorously branching bush with dark green, ovate leaves, from May on white flowers, from July on red or green seed pods. Annual.

Taste: Very piquant (spicy, hot).

Use: In stew, chili, and other spicy meat dishes.

Garden Culture: Start on the windowsill; beginning mid-May plant strong seedlings outdoors in a sunny spot in well fertilized soil. Use a separate bed; do not plant in herb garden. In a cool summer, peppers will only form in a foil tunnel

Pot Culture: Miniature peppers thrive better. Outdoor plants may be used in balcony boxes.

Harvest: Peppers in July/August. Dry slowly in shade. Green peppers will often turn red.

Storage: In screw-top jars, in vinegar or oil, or hung on thread.

Coriander

Chinese parsley
Coriandrum sativum

Appearance: Stems up to 27 in (70 cm) tall with leaves that are three-lobed on the lower plant and pinnate on the upper. White-pink flower umbels from June. Seeds brown and bipartite. Annual.

Taste: Spicy-sweet.

Use: Seeds in gingerbread, in pickling, Oriental sweet dishes, liqueur.

Garden Culture: Sow beginning of April in a very sunny spot. Lightly lime soil. Thin to stand 6 in (15 cm) apart. Maintain loose soil.

Harvest: Before the seeds are fully ripe, cut the stalk with blossoms in damp weather, dry, shake seeds out over a clean cloth.

Storage: In screw-topped jars.

Anethum graveolens

Appearance: Stems up to nearly 6 in (15 cm) tall, with very finely pinnate light green leaves. From June on large yellow flower umbels, seeds brown. Annual.

Taste: Leaves freshly spicy; seeds like caraway.

Use: Leaves in green, tomato, cucumber, and potato salads, sauces, fish. Seeds and umbels for pickling, etc.

Garden Culture: Sow in April, then every four weeks, in a sunny spot. Will not tolerate dryness.

Pot Culture: Between flowers in boxes on a balcony; in a pot on the windowsill it will become slightly yellow.

Harvest: Fresh leaves constantly; seeds from August on.

Storage: Leaves dried or frozen. Seeds in screw-top jars.

Foeniculum vulgare

Appearance: Oval stems up to 6 in (15 cm) tall with very finely dissected dark green leaves. From June with yellow flower umbels and brown ellipsoid seeds. Annual.

Taste: Aromatic and anise-like.

Use: Generally, the base of the plant is sliced and used as a salad green. The leaves and seeds may also be used as an anise flavoring.

Garden Culture: Sow seeds in April in a sunny place that will sometimes be shaded. Will burn in June sun and does not tolerate dryness.

Pot Culture: Plant in window boxes between other plants.

Harvest: Whole plants in window boxes for salad use. Also pick leaves continuously, and later mature seeds.

Storage: Leaves dried or frozen; seeds dried in screw-top jars.

Garlic

Allium sativum

Appearance: Bulb with many small "cloves," white or pink, depending on variety. Small leaves. A flower in a pointed sheath forms on the long stem. The sheath is twisted at first and thin and pointed when mature. Seed bulblets are located between the flowers. Annual.

Taste: Sharp.

Use: In almost all dishes, salads, pickles. When crushed, very powerful, milder when cut. Do not cook too long, or it loses taste.

Garden Culture: Plant cloves in August in a very sunny spot. The bulbs will be larger than if planted in the spring. Prepare soil with compost only.

Harvest: In summer when fall-planted; in fall when spring-planted.

Storage: Dry bulbs and store in a cool place. Cloves may be stored in oil.

Brassica hirta, B. nigra (shown in picture)

Appearance: Squarish stems, up to 47 in (1.20 m) tall, with rough, hairy, ovate leaves. Yellow flower racemes at the ends of shoots. Seeds of white mustard yellowish, of black mustard dark brown. Annual.

Taste: Sharp, spicy.

Use: Seeds for pickling cucumbers, tomatoes, etc.; for prepared mustard. Leaves in salad.

Garden Culture: Sow from the middle of May outdoors; germinates very quickly. Seeds ripen only in very sunny locations and with early sowing.

Pot Culture: Sow in ordinary potting soil.

Harvest: Young leaves continually. Cut seed stalks in damp weather; dry in oven at 125°F (51°C) for 1–2 hours.

Storage: Seeds in paper bags; in glass there is risk of sprouting.

Tall Nasturtium, Indian Cress
Tropaeolum majus

Appearance: Bushy or trailing plant with round, blue-green leaves and light orange to yellow flowers. Annual.

Taste: Cress-like but not so sharp.

Use: Leaves and flowers in salad, cottage cheese dishes, on bread and butter; flower buds (not the fruits!) as capers.

Garden Culture: Sow in mid-May in a sunny or semi-shady spot; plant deep. Works well at the edge of the garden; interplanted with potatoes imparts a special aroma.

Pot Culture: Pretty balcony plant, as underplanting for container plants. Do not fertilize heavily. Sensitive to direct sun and heat.

Harvest: From June on leaves and flowers; in spring flower buds.

Storage: Buds in brine as capers.

Pepperwort, tonguegrass
Lepidum sativum

Appearance: Tender, thin stems with light green variously pinnate leaflets. Flowers whitish pink. Annual.

Taste: Sharp, fresh, mildly peppery.

Use: Small plants only for salads, soups, cottage cheese, eggs.

Garden Culture: Sow from March on in rows or broadcast in garden; intersow between slower-growing plants until May and after August. Germinates in a few days; can be cut after 1 week. When used for interplanting, do not allow to grow taller than 4 in (10 cm) because the mustard oil contained in the peppergrass will inhibit the other plants.

Pot Culture: Grows without difficulty in shallow dishes lined with damp paper towel as with alfalfa sprouts.

Harvest: Fresh, constantly once it has attained height of 4–6 in (10–15 cm).

Pusley
Portulaca oleracea

Appearance: Fleshy stems with thick, obovate leaves. At the ends of shoots and in the branch axils tiny yellow flowers. Annual.

Taste: Fresh, tart.

Use: Leaves, stems, and flowers in salads of all kinds. Cooked like spinach.

Garden Culture: From the middle of May sow in rows in a sunny place every 3 weeks. Light germinator. May be fertilized only with compost! Water plentifully. Does not thrive in a cool summer.

Pot Culture: In sandy soil in wide pots or boxes. Do not fertilize, keep in a very bright place.

Harvest: 4 weeks after sowing, then continually. Do not cut back too far, or it will not continue to grow.

Satureja hortensis

Appearance: Branching, hard stems with small, dark green leaves and pink to lavender flowers. Annual.

Taste: Strong spicy-peppery.

Use: For green and dried beans, stews, potato dishes.

Garden Culture: From April in cold frame; from May outdoors in a sunny spot, best at the edge of the bean rows; protects beans from aphids. If allowed to stand too close together it develops few leaves. Needs light to germinate.

Pot Culture: With other herbs in flats.

Harvest: From June shortly before and during the blooming period if you're going to store, otherwise fresh.

Storage: As bouquet garni; in screw-top jars.

Sweet Marjoram

Annual marjoram
Origanum majorana

Appearance: Reddish, square stems with many branchings and fine, hairy, small, ovate leaves. From June whitish purple flowers. Annual.

Taste: Strong, spicy.

Use: Leaflets and flowers in fish dishes, fried potatoes, stew, tomato dishes.

Garden Culture: Start indoors (germinates in light); set out from May on in a very warm, sunny spot. Extremely susceptible to frost.

Pot Culture: In fall place 3–4 small plants together in one pot and set in a sunny window.

Harvest: Tips of branches constantly. For drying, cut whole branches shortly before blooming.

Storage: In a small linen bag or screw-top jar.

Carum carvi

Appearance: Up to 47 in (1.20 m) tall, squared, grooved stems with delicately pinnate leaves. From May white or pink flower umbels; from June with bipartite fruits. Biennial.

Taste: Sweetly aromatic.

Use: Ripe seeds and young leaves for cabbage dishes, cottage cheese dishes, potato dishes.

Garden Culture: Sow from April or in September in a sunny place, in damp, lightly fertilized ground. Germinates in light. In first year only leaf rosettes; in second year flowers and fruits.

Pot Culture: Only annual; use only leaves.

Harvest: Let seeds ripen; remove in damp weather; dry in oven.

Storage: Seeds in screw-top jar.

Apium graveolens

Appearance: Root and vegetable plant. Forms thick, white bulbs with squared stems and pinnate, dark green leaves. Cut celery is taken only to the root. Biennial, but not pleasant in second year.

Taste: Spicy.

Use: In soups, sauces, meat dishes.

Garden Culture: Start on the windowsill, as plant is very frost-sensitive. Germinates in light. From May on set out in favorable place. After growth achieved, fertilize.

Pot Culture: Only celery for cutting. Sow in a pot or flat from March on; keep damp.

Harvest: Young leaves constantly; a small amount needed because of powerful aroma. With root celery, only the outer leaves.

Storage: Pickling, freezing, drying.

Parsley

Petroselinum crispum

Appearance: In first year squared stems with curly feathered leaves in a rosette. In second year greenish-yellow flowers; leaves then unpleasant. Commercially available varieties are curly, smooth (Italian), and turnip-rooted parsley. Biennial.

Taste: Spicy.

Use: In salads, potatoes, vegetables, soups, sauces. Turnip-rooted parsley is cooked in soups and in meat dishes.

Garden Culture: Sow in summer when warm, in earth enriched with compost in part-shade. Change location every year; does not tolerate resowing in same soil. The more often one takes leaves, the more vigorously it grows.

Pot Culture: Sow anytime; buy young plants.

Harvest: Fresh constantly.

Storage: Freeze.

Spoonwort
Cochlearia officinalis

Appearance: Up to 15½ in (40 cm) high, square, grooved stems with spoon-shaped leaves below, ovate leaves above. From May to June in second year fragrant, white flower racemes. Biennial.

Taste: Cress-like, salty.

Use: In all salads, especially potato salad, in cottage cheese, and on bread and butter. Only use raw.

Garden Culture: Sow from March on or September outdoors in rows in a semishaded spot. Germinates within 2 weeks. Maintain good moisture. In winter cover with branches to prevent freezing and to keep on harvesting.

Pot Culture: Sow anytime in potting soil; always keep well dampened.

Harvest: All year, only the lower spoon-shaped leaves.

Angelica

Archangel, wild parsnip
Angelica archangelica

Appearance: Roots resemble those of the horseradish—long, thick, and many-branched. Large, pinnate leaves with thick leaf sheaths on hollow stems up to 8 ft (2.50 m) tall. In July semicircular greenish flower umbels. Perennial.

Taste: Musky, spicy.

Use: Leaves and stems in soups, sauces, salads. Roots in liqueur.

Garden Culture: Sow in fall in humus soil with added compost. Plants require great deal of space in semishade. Dies after 4 years in same spot.

Harvest: Fresh leaves all summer; roots in late fall.

Storage: Leaves dried, stems and roots in closed jars.

Lauris nobilis

Appearance: Sturdy shrub with leathery, dark green, linear leaves. From May on older plants small, white, fragrant blossoms. Evergreen shrub.

Taste: Spicy.

Use: In meat dishes, stews, included in pickles.

Pot Culture: Thrives in areas as far north as New Jersey as a container plant; is often formed into a tree or a pyramid. Needs half garden soil, half compost in a sufficiently large pot. In summer water daily when outdoors; the plant's leaves will fall if it dries out. In winter keep in a bright, cool room. Prune into shape in fall. Water sparingly.

Harvest: Fresh leaves constantly. They are more aromatic dried (after cutting back in fall).

Storage: Dried in bags.

Oswego tea, Monarda
Monarda didyma

Appearance: Angular, sturdy stems with pointed, toothed leaves. From June on decorative red flowers, which appear in whorls in layers on the stem. Perennial rootstock.
Taste: Like mint.
Use: Leaves in fruit salads, jellies, fresh fruit juices, iced tea, cold drinks.
Garden Culture: Seedlings in well-composted soil in a sunny or semishaded spot. Remove flower buds in first year so plants will be bushier. Propagate by root division.
Harvest: Fresh leaves from June. Shortly before blooming for drying.
Storage: In screw-top jars.

Garden burnet
Sanguisorba minor

Appearance: Small pinnate, toothed, green leaflets grow very densely in a broad rosette. From May reddish round flowers on long stems. Perennial.

Taste: Fresh, somewhat like cucumbers.

Use: In salad, egg dishes, sauces (herb sauce).

Garden Culture: Sow in March in rows in a very sunny place; later thin to stand 8 in (20 cm) apart. Cut out flower stems to induce more leaves. Plants sow themselves throughout whole garden. After 2 years bed should be reseeded.

Harvest: The fresh bright green leaves constantly; the older ones do not have flavor and are hard.

Allium schoenoprasum

Appearance: Long, thin, green, tube-like leek leaves grow from many tiny bulbs. In July pink pseudo-umbels on hard stems. Perennial.
Taste: Sharp, flavor similar to onions.
Use: In salads, soups, cottage cheese, omelettes, potatoes, sauces.
Garden Culture: Sow in April or in August, in limey, humus soil, semishade. Divide in fall.

Pot Culture: Dig up bulblets in fall; allow to dry; plant in potting soil in February; do not allow to dry out but don't keep too damp. Do not place in the sun. After numerous cuttings, place in garden.
Harvest: Constantly all summer.
Storage: Deep freeze.

Rose geranium, lemon-scented geranium, peppermint geranium

Pelargonium graveolens/ citrosum/tomentosum

Appearance: Lemon-scented geraniums have three-lobed rough leaflets and mauve flowers; rose geraniums have rough, coarse leaves and pink flowers; peppermint geraniums have soft, trailing tendrils, grass-green leaves, and white flowers. Perennial.

Taste: Like roses, lemons, peppermint.

Use: In jellies, liqueurs, sweet dishes, sparingly in exotic salads.

Pot Culture: Fragrant geraniums are not standard items commercially. If you get a cutting, root in a not-too-rich soil-sand mixture, then continue to fertilize and water like geraniums, preferably on a balcony in summer and in a sunny window in winter.

Harvest: Constantly fresh.

Hyssop

Hyssopus officinalis

Appearance: Squarish, woody stems up to 15½ in (40 cm) high with small, linear, dark green leaves arranged in whorls around the stem. In July blue or (rarely) white flowers at the leaf axis. Perennial.

Taste: Spicy, somewhat like mint.

Use: In salad, beans, soups, veal stew, punches. In small quantities only.

Garden Culture: Young plants in loose, alkaline soil in a warm, sunny place; appropriate for a small garden. Protect from frost in winter.

Harvest: Young shoots and leaves continually. For drying during the blooming period.

Storage: Immediately after drying in tightly closed jars; otherwise, there is a risk of losing flavor.

Juniperus communis

Appearance: Evergreen shrub up to 10 ft (3 m) high with very prickly, blue-green leaves (needles). The small round fruits are green the first year; the second year they become blue with a light bloom. Perennial.

Use: Blue fruits only, for game, sauerkraut, fish, and liqueur.

Garden Culture: Handsome miniature shrub. Needs sandy, alkaline soil and very sunny location.

Pot Culture: Small specimens as container plants in deep pots (taproot).

Harvest: The blue berries from October (wear gloves).

Storage: After careful drying or baking in screw-top jars.

Common balm, bee balm, sweet balm

Melissa officinalis

Appearance: Squarish, hairy, branching stems with toothed, light green leaves growing from root runners. From July on there are small white to light blue flowers. Perennial.

Taste: Fresh like lemon, bittersweet.

Use: In salads, sauces, on tomatoes, as tea.

Garden Culture: Sow mid-May in a sunny spot, or, preferably plant seedlings in May. Very undemanding, spreads throughout garden. Cut back in fall.

Pot Culture: Young plants for 1 year in a sunny window or on a balcony, then in garden.

Harvest: Constantly from May on, only the young, small leaves. Cut for drying shortly before or during blooming period.

Storage: Dried in screw-top jar.

Levisticum officinale

Appearance: Up to 5 ft (1.5 m) high, full shrub with sturdy, pinnate, almost triangular leaves. From July small yellow-green flower umbels. In spring the first shoots are red. Perennial.

Taste: Strong, spicy, somewhat like celery.

Use: A small amount only in soups, meat dishes, stews, salads. Can be cooked.

Garden Culture: Sow in April or August; better to set out seedlings in soil well furnished with compost. Plants remain all year, but need space and semishade.

Pot Culture: One-year-old plants only; all pots become too small for older ones.

Harvest: Fresh leaves from May to November.

Storage: Dried, pickled.

Felon herb
Artemisia vulgaris

Appearance: Tall bush, up to 79 in (2 m), with hairy stems and varyingly pinnate leaves with dark green upper sides and whitish undersides. From July to September yellowish hairy flowers in large open clusters. Perennial.

Taste: Herb-spicy, slightly bitter.

Use: In all fatty meat dishes.

Garden Culture: Seedlings in a sunny, very warm place with very meager soil (mixed with sand or gravel). Allow to freeze in winter; comes back in spring.

Harvest: Leaves, as long as plant is not blooming; afterwards they are too bitter.

Storage: Dried in screw-top jars.

Oregano

Pot marjoram, wild marjoram, origano, origany
Origanum vulgare

Appearance: Up to 20 in (50 cm) long, woody, reddish stems with small, finely haired, gray-green leaflets. From July pink fascicles of flowers at the tips. Perennial.

Taste: Herb-spicy.

Use: For all Mediterranean dishes, cheese, meat, soups, sauces, sausage.

Garden Culture: Sow in April in the warmest place in the garden (the sunnier and warmer the better the taste). Preferably, set out a young plant. Plants grow quickly. Completely winter-hardy.

Pot Culture: In deep, wide pots on the balcony, winter protection.

Harvest: Fresh leaves constantly from June on; for drying, on a sunny day while in bloom.

Storage: As bouquet garni, in screw-top jar, in oil.

Mentha piperita

Appearance: Up to 27 in (70 cm) long, reddish, squarish stems with dark green to reddish leaflets. From July pink tight clusters of flowers. Perennial.

Taste: Strong, freshly aromatic, cooling.

Use: In tea, summer drinks, liqueur.

Garden Culture: Young plants from May in a shady place with damp soil that is rich in compost. Containment in a basin with no bottom is advisable.

Pot Culture: Young plants on the balcony; in winter inside in a kitchen window. Try other varieties such as pineapple, spicy, or orange mint.

Harvest: Fresh leaves from June on; for drying, just before blooming.

Storage: In screw-top jars, in bags.

Rosmarinus officinalis

Appearance: Up to 39 in (1 m) high, very woody shrub with small, blue-green, needle-like leaves which are white underneath. Blue labiate flowers from March on. Perennial. Strong scent.

Taste: Herby, bitter, aromatic.

Use: In Mediterranean dishes, roasts, fowl, cheese, sauces.

Garden Culture: Seedlings from mid-May in a sunny place. Best in a large pot that can be taken inside in winter.

Rosemary is not winter-hardy in northern climates. Keep well supplied with compost and moisture.

Pot Culture: From March on place outside in a sunny spot.

Harvest: Fresh shoots constantly, taking only as much as the plant can tolerate.

Common sage, garden sage
Salvia officinalis

Appearance: Sturdy, woody bush with somewhat wide-spreading branches with silvery; hairy, ovate leaves; greener in winter. From June, blue or purple flowers on long spikes. Perennial.

Taste: Strong, spicy, camphor-like.

Use: In meat, ham, poultry, cheese, fatty fish, Mediterranean stews, sauces.

Garden Culture: Young plants from May in a sunny place with loose, dry soil. Do not fertilize. Winter protection in more northern climates. Cut back somewhat in early fall.

Pot Culture: Maximum 2 years; try less common varieties, such as "Purpurascens" or "Tricolor."

Harvest: Young leaflets fresh. Cut shoot tips for drying.

Storage: Dried in screw-top jars, bags.

Sour dock
Rumex acetosa

Appearance: Reddish stems grow from one leaf rosette, 11½–31 in (30–80 cm) tall, with arrow-shaped, dark green to reddish leaves, and bright red flower panicles in May. Perennial.

Taste: Very sour.

Use: Leaves in soup, salads, spinach. Cook only briefly. Caution: Do not eat much raw Sorrel as it is high in oxalic acid!

Garden Culture: Cultivated plants have larger leaves than the wild form. Sow in May or August in humus soil or set out seedlings in their own bed. Thrives also in shade. Always break off flowers to encourage more leaves.

Pot Culture: Keep young plants in a deep pot of potting soil in a north window.

Harvest: Fresh young leaves continually; the old ones taste bitter.

Old man
Artemisia abrotanum

Appearance: Thick, up to 39 in (1 m) high bush with many finely pinnate leaflets on woody stems. Topmost shoots soft. Small, rounded, yellowish flowers on the ends of shoots. Perennial.

Taste: Like lemon, somewhat bitter.

Use: In sauces, salads, roasts. Use sparingly.

Garden Culture: Seedlings in a very sunny place. Keep soil dry. Can be propagated from branch tips. Cover in winter; cut back only slightly in spring.

Pot Culture: In a large plant container in a sunny place in summer, cool and bright in winter.

Harvest: Tips of shoots fresh. Dry during blooming period.

Storage: Dried leaves in screw-top jar, fresh in vinegar and oil.

Estragon
Artemisia dracunculus

Appearance: Up to 39 in (1 m) tall, branching stems with small, linear, dark green leaves; from June greenish flowers at tops of stem. Perennial.

Taste: Freshly spicy, bitter-sweet.

Use: In salads, fish, poultry, soups, sauces.

Garden Culture: *Russian tarragon* (not so delicately spicy) is sown from April on in a sunny, protected spot. *French tarragon* (much more aromatic) increases by means of root runners. Both varieties need much moisture, but no standing water! After 4 years replace plant with a new one.

Pot Culture: Young plants can be kept for 1 year in a very bright, warm window.

Harvest: The leaves constantly.

Storage: In vinegar (tarragon vinegar).

Common thyme
Thymus vulgaris

Appearance: Very woody, bushy stems with small, gray-green winter-hardy leaflets. Pink flowers from May. Perennial.

Taste: Very spicy.

Use: In fish dishes, stews, sauces, potatoes, poultry, game. Use only a little.

Garden Culture: Young plants in a very sunny spot, preferably in a rock garden. Needs thin, sandy, unfertilized soil. Keep dry. In early fall, cut back shoots. In cold regions give winter protection.

Pot Culture: Young plants during the summer on a balcony; in winter in a sunny window.

Harvest: Fresh small shoots constantly. For drying in fall.

Storage: In screw-top jars, in vinegar or oil.

Nasturtium officinale

Appearance: Stems up to 15½ in (40 cm) long with juicy, green, coarsely pinnate leaves, with tiny roots on undersides. From May white blooms. Perennial.

Taste: Very sharp.

Use: In salads, cottage cheese, herb butter, on bread and butter.

Garden Culture: Sow in waterproof plastic saucer filled half with water, half with soil. The water level must always be ⅜ in (1 cm) above the soil. Place saucer in a shady place. Keep removing rooted pieces and replanting; old plants become unproductive. Keep cool for better growth.

Harvest: Old leaves continually; they are more aromatic than younger ones. Harvest until December.

Calamint
Satureja montana

Appearance: Up to 19½ in (50 cm) tall. Small dark green leaves on branching stems that rapidly become woody; white, pink, or purple labiate flowers in between leaves from June on. Perennial.

Taste: Like annual savory but somewhat stronger.

Use: In beans, soups, potato dishes, stews.

Garden Culture: Sow in April or August in a sunny place. Plant seedlings in May. Keep dry. Cut back somewhat in spring.

Pot Culture: Shelter even in winter in a balcony flower box.

Harvest: Flavor is strongest just before and during the blooming period (flowers can also be used). Older plants only, all winter.

Storage: As a bouquet, dried.

The use of herbs and spices is as old as civilization. Herbs have always been used to increase the pleasure of food and drink, as well as to preserve life and health. The more highly developed the culture, the more refined its use of herbs and, therefore, the more important herbs and spices were as items of trade. Spices had to be brought from the Orient, no matter what the cost. And it did cost—often, spices were more expensive than gold and precious jewels. The local herbs that cost little or nothing were left to the simple folk. The poor could not afford doctors, but herbs helped cure many ailments. In addition, herbs made meager fare taste better.

The story of seasonings is fascinating and reaches far back into the past. Archaeologists have found that even in the Stone Age herbs were used for seasoning. Before our ancestors had ever discovered fire, they had discovered herbs. Laurel, thyme, and caraway are described on the 6000-year-old clay tablets of the Sumerians. Four-thousand-year-old wall paintings in Crete show coriander, celery, and mint, and a 3500-year-old papyrus from an Egyptian grave contains almost 800 recipes using herbs and spices.

Especially in the Mediterranean regions, the seasoning herbs have always played an important role. People procured valuable spices from the Orient over a 3000-mile-long spice route. Egypt became rich through this trade in costly spices. When the Queen of Sheba went to visit King Solomon she did not take gold and jewels as a present, but spices. The ancient Romans used them so freely in their cooking that learned men and those skilled in medicine warned against immoderate use. Roman beauties perfumed themselves with marjoram and mint, and even the legionaires smelled of herbs.

In the North, over the Alps, herbs were chiefly valued as medicine. Priests and herb-women knew how to handle them skillfully; and many an herbalist was burned as a witch or a sorcerer during the Inquisition. When Charlemagne, in his decree *Capitulare de villis*, proclaimed first to his tenants, later to all the peasantry, what they had to plant in their gardens, healing and seasoning herbs were also included. From amaranth to wood mint, the emperor's list contained some 89 herbs. Traveling monks brought strange seasoning herbs from the Roman Empire to the North. Rosemary and coriander were introduced in farm gardens.

In the 18th and 19th centuries cooking herbs again became very fashionable. The more artfully the seasonings were used in her kitchen, the higher the reputation of a metropolitan housewife, and a kitchen garden full of herbs was an absolute must. This custom began to die by the beginning of the 20th century. Old traditions did not fit in with the emerging Industrial Age. The beneficent discoveries of medicine made the healing herbs superfluous. People also renounced the fragrant seasoning herbs in the kitchen until the precious treasure of the herbs was rediscovered a few years ago. Then they had to learn all over again how to use them skillfully.

Herbs in the Garden

Seeds and Seedlings

If you want to grow cooking herbs in your own garden, you have two options: Sow them yourself or buy young plants. *Annual and biennial herbs* can be sown directly in the garden. Cold-sensitive herbs, like basil and marjoram, and very slowly germinating herbs, like parsley, are better bought as seedlings at a nursery or started on the windowsill or in a small greenhouse or coldframe. There is a great choice of herb seeds in garden centers and seed catalogs, but you can also harvest seeds yourself and store them dried over the winter. Many herbs are *light germinators;* that is, they require light to germinate. When they are sown they are only scattered on the soil and lightly covered with sand. You can also leave them uncovered, if it is possible to keep the birds away from them. *Dark germinators,* on the other hand, must be placed in the soil at a depth of at least 4 times the diameter of the seed. *Perennial* herbs are better planted as seedlings. If you buy them from a nursery, they are usually in small plastic pots and are well rooted. These container plants can be planted at any time of year—the best time, of course, is spring, after the last frost.

Raising Them Yourself

It's fun to raise a selection of cooking herbs on the windowsill. You then have strong seedlings for the garden early in the season and can also have an early harvest of the frost-sensitive herbs. Basil, for instance, does not germinate at temperatures under 59°F (15°C). A small window greenhouse, a shallow wooden flat, or some flowerpots will do for a windowsill garden. The drainage hole in the bottom of the flowerpot should be covered with a piece of broken pot, the flat lined with plastic wrap, or the floor of the window greenhouse spread with a thin layer of sand for drainage. Then add special seed-starting mix or potting soil that you have mixed with an equal quantity of clean sand. Spread the seeds thinly over the soil. Cover the dark germinators with sand or soil, light germinators with a piece of paper or a thin layer of sand. After planting, water very carefully, preferably with a sprayer. With a window greenhouse, the transparent cover is now closed. The flat can be covered with a piece of glass or a piece of transparent wrap; if using flowerpots, place a piece of glass over them or fasten a plastic bag over them with a rubber band. This develops a forcing climate in which the seeds will be sure to germinate. As soon as the first leaflets show, remove the coverings for 10 minutes twice a day so that the plants will get air. When the seedlings are ¾ in (2 cm) high, carefully remove them from the starting container and replant them in groups of 2 or 3 in a new pot. Now you no longer need to cover them. In an east or west window they will grow into sturdy young plants that you can set outdoors in May after the last frost, or set out on a balcony in a box or pot, or continue to grow on the windowsill.

Sowing and Planting Outdoors

If you are sowing directly outside, the ground must be prepared first. The herb garden should be mostly free of weeds that can overgrow hardy wild herbs or tender seedlings. Then hoe the area thoroughly—do not dig up!—break up large clods of earth and rake the ground smooth.

Sow annual herbs in rows; you can then distinguish more easily between the sprouting herbs and the weeds. Place a little rich compost in the furrow, then the seeds. Afterward, depending on whether the seeds germinate in light or darkness, cover them with some sand (also bran to keep off snails) or with soil, and gently water. Until the seedlings become strong, the garden should not be allowed to dry out. Do not forget to put labels at the end of each row! The later in the spring you sow herbs, the sooner you will have success. As a rule, herb seeds do not like any cold or wet ground. Biennial herbs can also be sown in early fall. Seedlings can be planted outdoors after mid-May. In the hole in the prepared soil place only one handful of compost. Only lovage and chives need additional fertilizer. Press the seedlings in firmly, and water. In the first few days you must water more often until the plants are well established. After that they should be kept somewhat dry.

The Herb Garden
Almost all kitchen herbs are happiest in a very sunny garden. There are some exceptions: Dill prefers to grow between cucumbers or other plants, where it has cool roots but a great deal of sun on leaves and flowers. Summer savory belongs in the bean field, where it keeps the aphids off the beans. Borage is too large for the herb garden, but it quickly fills in the gaps left by harvesting in the vegetable garden. Garden nasturtium is sown on the edges of the vegetable garden or in the miniature garden. Peppergrass is sown in its own garden or between lettuce and potatoes. All other herbs belong in the herb garden, which must be in full sun. Do not plant the herbs too close together; they will grow bigger than you think and should not take light and nutrients away from one another. Separate annuals and other herbs, which will simplify the work in the garden. Large plants that grow tall should be on the north side of the garden, the small ones on the south. Planted thus, the big ones will not deprive the small ones of the precious sunlight. In a spiral planting, each plant has a sunny place.

The Soil Requirements of Herbs
With few exceptions, herbs prefer loose, sandy, dry ground. In a garden where the soil is rich and heavy, you have to loosen it with plenty of sand. In a garden with standing water, the herbs may even need drainage of gravel or tile shards. Build a high bed for your herb collection if your garden soil is too wet. It is unnecessary, even harmful, to fertilize in an herb garden. Although too much fertilizer allows the plant to shoot up, the aromatic component is lost. Thus, the more meager the herb garden soil is, the better. With sandy soil add some crushed stone in seed furrows and plant holes and, in addition, in spring the garden should receive only one large shovelful of well-decomposed compost per square yard (square meter). It should be spread thinly over the surface of the garden and hoed in.

Care of the Herbs
An herb garden does not require much work. Weeds should not get the upper hand or the herbs will be deprived not only of sun

but of nutrients. If you do not wish to give perennial herbs compost in the spring, you can fertilize them when shoots appear with a broth of stinging nettles (nettles and water left to ferment for a week, strained, and thinned 1:10 with water, and poured on the roots).

The herb garden need only be watered during long dry spells. Insects and disease do not often appear; if they do, however, you should attempt to combat them only with natural means;

So that parsley is not infested with nematodes, it should never be sown or planted twice in the same place. If dill does not thrive, try it in another location. Peppermint rust appears if the plants are too close; if they are attacked, cut back the shoots radically. Snails often eat sprouting herb seeds. Strew the seed furrows thinly with wheat or barley bran. In the fall severely cut back perennial herbs. Exceptions: Thyme, rosemary, bay, and sage are pruned only for shape so that they will be many-branched and bushy the following spring. One can continue to harvest from these herbs all winter. In regions with harsh climates most perennial herbs need winter protection. Cover them with pine boughs or a layer of straw.

Harvesting Herbs from the Garden

Fresh leaves and shoots of all the kitchen herbs can be picked from spring until fall. Naturally, if the herbs are ready to use fresh, you need only pick as much as you are going to use in cooking. Even if you place freshly cut herbs in a glass of water, they quickly lose their aroma. If herb leaves are to be preserved for the winter, they must be harvested when they have the strongest scent and when thorough cutting of the plant will no longer harm it. For the plants in this book, these harvest times are given in the notes about the particular plant. Usually it is midsummer, shortly before or during the blooming period. Harvest the herbs for storage on a sunny day around noon. If the leaves and branches are picked when they are still damp, they can get moldy, even with the most careful handling. Also, the smell is stronger when the herbs are picked in dry, warm weather.

With most perennial herbs the entire shoot is cut off just above the ground. Exceptions: Rosemary, bay thyme, and sage. With these herbs, cut branches back only about one-third, because they do not branch from the root but will put out new shoots. When you want to harvest seeds—for instance, coriander, dill, caraway, or mustard—you must observe the plants. Shortly before ripening (the seeds become brown but do not drop by themselves), cut the blossom along with the stem. Bind these into a loose bouquet and hang them up over a clean cloth. They will continue to ripen while they are drying and from time to time seeds will fall onto the cloth. When finished, tap the bouquet on the cloth so that the last seeds fall out. Then lay the seeds in a shallow saucer, shake them slightly, and gently blow away the dried leaves and other plant parts.

When you are harvesting roots, you should wait as long as possible. Even in October the roots are still growing stronger. At the end of October carefully dig out the roots with a spading fork. This is no problem in sandy soil but in heavier soils the roots are taken from the ground after a rainy day. Of course it takes some trouble to clean the roots of the soil that clings to them, but they do not break off as easily as they do in hard-baked dry ground.

Herbs in Boxes and Pots

If you do not have a garden, you can still raise herbs. You can grow many kitchen herbs well on a balcony in flats, small wooden boxes, and in pots. The plants spend the summer outdoors; in winter take the perennials indoors and continue to harvest small quantities. Annuals and biennials are sown in boxes and pots the same way they are sown in the garden. They germinate well and when they are harvested, you can sow again. You can also keep your perennial plants in pots and boxes. After 2 years they become too large for the cramped root space. Bay, rosemary, and juniper can remain in pots all year.

Location for Balcony and Indoor Herbs

Like those in the garden, cooking herbs on the balcony and indoors need the warmest possible place. On a balcony you should not hang the herb boxes on the railing like petunias and geraniums, but put them in a sunny, protected place along the house wall. In the house the kitchen window is ideal only if it faces west or east, so that it has sufficient light and warmth. North windows are unsuitable for herbs, and only the most sun-loving herbs can be kept in a south window; herbs with thin leaves will burn there. An absolute must: Herbs that are kept indoors must be placed outside in summer. If you do not have a balcony, stand them securely on the outer windowsill. Plants will develop their good aroma only in this way.

What Kind of Box or Pot?

Flower boxes are handy for raising every possible kitchen herb on a balcony. Annual plants that are cut frequently (for instance, peppergrass, mustard, basil) are better sown in shallow wooden flats. Large clay pots are better for perennial herbs. Nasturtiums can even serve as a floral decoration for the balcony. Inside on the windowsill, plastic flowerpots are practical because the potting medium does not dry out so quickly. Of course, clay pots look better. A suggestion: Set several plastic pots with different herbs in a pretty, shallow ceramic bowl whose interior you have lined with peat moss.

Soil and Fertilizer

Before planting or sowing kitchen herbs in pots and boxes, always spread a thin drainage layer of sand on the bottom of the container, even in the smallest pot. It prevents dangerous standing water. Because almost all herbs thrive best in rather poor soil, the previously fertilized, commercial potting soil is not the best medium for them. If at all possible, you should mix the soil for kitchen herbs yourself. The recipe is: ⅓ well-rotted compost, ⅓ sand, and ⅓ peat. Alternatively, you can use TKS 1 (a weakly fertilized prepared potting medium) mixed with ⅓ sand. Mix some bone meal into the potting medium, about 1 teaspoon in an ordinary flowerpot. Bone meal supplies nutrients to the plants very slowly over months, and you will not have to fertilize for the rest of the summer. In winter, when the herbs are in the house, they should receive a weak dose of fertilizer every 4 weeks, preferably guano liquid fertilizer. Plants on the balcony and indoors must be watered more often than those in the garden because the soil dries out faster, but never allow the soil in the pot or box to remain soaking wet.

Harvesting from Pot and Box

The yield from pots and boxes is not as abundant as that from the garden. Take only as much as you need to use fresh each day. The annual herbs do not have much room to thrive, and the perennials will not become old enough to be very large. With these you always cut off only a little anyway—if possible, the ends of branches. In time this will have the effect of making them beautifully bushy. Only those gardeners who use very large plant containers can harvest enough from balcony and houseplants for drying.

How to Store Your Harvest

Many kitchen herbs can be dried, but there are also other good ways of storing, such as freezing, salting, and covering with vinegar or oil.

Drying

If you have an airy, dry place that is protected from the sun, you can dry your kitchen herbs there. This can be a protected spot on the balcony, the attic, or a little-used room in the house. Under no circumstances should herbs be dried in the sun because this will destroy the fragrance. Drying in high humidity is a problem because the drying process is retarded, which results in loss of fragrance and risk of mold.

The harvested herbs are bound into bouquets; with a rubber band the stems stay together more securely even after they have dried. Hang the bunch of herbs head down. When they are rustling dry, take the bunch down, pick the flowers from the stems or cut the whole branch into tiny pieces. Store the dried herbs in tins or screw-top jars.

Dessicating

You can also dry herbs in a dessicator or in an oven. This is especially recommended if you do not have a good drying place or if the herbs must be washed before drying. In areas where air pollution is high this is often unavoidable. After washing, pat the herbs dry with paper towels. Then lay them loosely and not too thickly on a baking pan covered with aluminum foil or baking paper. Dry out the herbs in an oven at 125°F (51°C). The oven door must be left slightly open while they are drying. It is best if you place the handle of a cooking spoon between oven and door. After drying, allow the herbs to cool, then pull them apart and store in jars or tins. Dessicating is simpler in a dessicator. Temperature and length of time are indicated; however, it is always advisable to allow some additional time.

Drying Seeds and Roots

You should also dry harvested seeds in the oven after they've fallen from the flower heads. Then they will not rot. Half an hour at 125°F (51°C) is enough to render the seeds storable. Wash roots clean after harvesting and dry them. Very thick roots should be cut into finger thicknesses; smaller ones are dried whole. Using a thick needle, thread them onto a string, which you then hang in the same type of place as the bunch of herbs. You can also dry roots in the oven or the dessicator. They must not become hard, however; they must be completely dry. Keep checking them throughout the drying process.

Freezing

You can also freeze many herbs. A tried and true method: Cut freshly harvested herbs as small as possible. Put them in an ice cube tray with very little water, and freeze. Place the frozen herb cubes in labeled containers in the freezer. This way you get only a small quantity of herbs whenever you need them. Another method: Quickly freeze the herbs, uncut, with stems, leaves, and flowers. Then squeeze the frozen herbs into a bag and store them in the freezer. This way you avoid the tiresome mincing operation. You can also freeze ready-to-use herb mixtures: For instance, the herbs for the green sauce, soup herbs, Provencal mixtures, Italian salad herb mixtures, and so on. It is also possible to freeze the fresh herbs and vegetables together.

Preserving in Vinegar and Oil

In oil and vinegar you do not retain the herbs, only their aroma. Depending on your preference, you can season many dishes with these essences. For preservation in vinegar or in oil pick the herbs at the point when their fragrance is at its best—in the midday hours of a warm day. With some herbs the flowers intensify the fragrance. Thoroughly wash and dry the stems, leaves, and flowers, and place the herbs loosely in bottles or jars. In bottles you can use the whole stem, which looks very decorative; in jars the herbs can be cut only into large pieces. Then pour in just enough vinegar or oil to completely cover the herb. Vinegar used for preserving should not be too young, otherwise a "mother" will form between the herb branches. A good wine vinegar or a 2-year-old apple cider vinegar is suitable for this purpose. If you are preserving herbs in oil, it is best to use a good olive oil because this will not become rancid. Cap the bottles and jars. Then place the bottles and jars with herb vinegar and herb oil in a warm place for 2–4 weeks; you may even place the vinegar bottles in the warm sun! After this the liquid will have completely taken on the aroma of the herb and may be stored in a dark place. The herbs can remain in the liquid, which looks very attractive.

Salting

Herbs that are going to be used as flavorings for sauces, soups, and stews can also be preserved in salt. Thoroughly wash the leaves of the herb plant, do not cut them too small, and layer them alternately with salt in a jar or a stoneware crock with a cover. The proportions should always be 5 parts herb to 1 part salt. Press the mixture well down with the handle of a cooking spoon. Salted herbs will keep in a cool place for an entire year.

Herbs in the Kitchen

The secret of the right herbs is simple: The herbs should enhance the taste of the dish, not overwhelm it. If there are several herbs or spices in a dish, you have to use them in a subtle way so that they do not conflict with each other. One herb is always dominant; the others may only round it out. If you are using very powerful herbs, like lovage or garlic, use them very sparingly—you should be trying to achieve a particular garlic or lovage flavor. Fresh herbs can be minced fine or added in small bunches to the dish; dried herbs may be crumbled or cooked with the dish in small gauze bags (bouquets garnis).

Salads

Add fresh, minced, or torn herbs to the dressing and allow them to remain for 10–30 minutes. Only then are the salad vegetables added. Garnish green salads with herb flowers.
Some popular herbs for salads are basil, chives, dill, garlic, marjoram, mustard powder, oregano, rosemary or thyme.

Sauces

Cook herbs in hot sauces for fish, meat, poultry, and vegetables. In cold sauces, add the herbs at the end of the preparation time. They must then be allowed to steep for 1–2 hours. When ground in a mortar, they release their odors with special intensity.

Soups

For clear soups of meat, fish, and poultry, add a bunch of herbs while they are cooking. Herb soups are prepared with a base of butter, some flour, and broth; the herbs are added at the end, after mincing or crushing.

For even more savory soups, try using aniseed, basil, bay leaves, bouquet garni, celery seed, chervil, chives, dill, fennel, fines herbes, lemon balm, marjoram, mustard powder, oregano, parsley, rosemary, sage, sorrel, or thyme.

Vegetables

These should be only improved by the addition of herbs, never overwhelmed. Each vegetable has its own special herb but it is certainly worthwhile to try out new vegetable-herb combinations. The following herbs are among those used with vegetables: aniseed, bouquet garni, chervil, coriander, dill, marjoram, mustard powder, rosemary, or thyme.

Meat Dishes

These are made more digestible with strong herbs and also gain a very typical flavor from spices and herbs. In meat dishes, herbs are used in marinades, rubbed into the meat, included as filling or herb covering, or simply added at the end in a sauce.

With beef, try bay leaves, bouquet garni, celery seed, coriander, garlic, marjoram, mustard, oregano, parsley, rosemary, sage, or thyme.

Caraway, dill, fennel, garlic, juniper berries, mustard powder, rosemary, sage, or savory will add flavor to pork.

When serving lamb, dill seed, garlic, mustard, rosemary, thyme can be used.

On poultry you might try basil, bouquet garni, coriander, fennel, garlic, lemon balm, rosemary, sage, sorrel, or thyme.

To add flavor to fish, try aniseed, basil, bay leaves, bouquet garni, celery seed, chervil, chives, dill weed, fennel, or parsley.

Desserts

Flavored with herbs, these are rendered especially piquant by the mixture of sweet and sharp, mild and strong. An instinct for herbs is especially important here.

Among those used are angelica, aniseed, basil, caraway, coriander, or fennel.

Teas

Specific herb teas are sometimes recommended for specific medical complaints. Summer teas of fresh herbs, well cooled, are considered by many to be the best and healthiest thirst-quenchers.

Liqueurs

Good liqueurs can be produced from herb mixtures as well as from individual spicy herbs. They should not be sweetened too much.

Spiced Wines

For an aperitif you can serve good, not too dry white or red wine that has been flavored with a handful of different herbs.

Herb Recipes

Pesto

3–5 large cloves garlic
2 C (½ L) basil
4 oz (100 g) grated Parmesan cheese
1 Tbsp pinenuts (can substitute sunflower seeds or coarsely
    chopped walnuts or hazelnuts)
½ C (⅛ L) oil
Beat oil with Parmesan until a thick paste develops. Crush garlic cloves and toasted pinenuts; mince basil; stir into mixture. All ingredients may also be placed in blender or food processor. Serve pesto with pasta.

Aioli

5 garlic cloves
2 egg yolks, slightly beaten
1 C (¼ L) olive oil
½ slice white bread
1 tsp vinegar
hot water
salt
Crush garlic cloves in mortar or with a garlic press; add a little salt. In a bowl place egg yolks, vinegar, and garlic. Beat in the oil drop by drop, as with mayonnaise. After half the oil is added, crumble in the bread, which has been softened in the hot water. Beat in remaining oil. Aioli is delicious with broiled meat and fish.

Chervil Soup

5¼ oz (150 g) fresh chervil
1 qt (1 L) beef broth or bouillon cube
2 Tbs butter
2 Tbs flour
2 egg yolks
1 C (¼ L) heavy cream
nutmeg
salt
lemon juice

Melt butter, stir in flour, and cook, stirring; add hot broth; stir smooth and bring to boil. Remove from heat; beat cream and egg together and stir into soup mixture. Season with salt, nutmeg, and lemon juice. Stir in minced chervil; let stand for several minutes. Serve with croutons (toasted white bread cubes).

Herb Sauce

About 5¼ oz (150 g) green herbs: parsley, chives, burnet, dill,
  borage, chervil, lemon balm (or others, according to taste)
1 onion
1 clove garlic
4 hard-boiled eggs
½ C (⅛ L) oil
1 C (¼ L) sour cream
mustard
salt
pepper

Beat egg yolk with oil until creamy. Stir in sour cream; add minced onion and minced garlic. Season with mustard, salt, and pepper to taste. Stir in the herbs, minced fine, and let sauce stand in the refrigerator for 30 minutes. Serve with boiled meat, fish, or baked potatoes.

Omelette aux fines herbes

3½ oz (100 g) each chives, parsley, chervil, tarragon, basil
5 eggs
some milk or cream
butter

Beat the eggs and milk with a wire whisk until well mixed. Melt butter; slide the egg mixture into the pan. Just before eggs are dry, sprinkle in the herbs, fold the omelette and allow to cook a

little while longer. The same recipe can also be used to make
herb pancakes.

Herb Mustard

2 oz (50 g) mustard seed
chervil, tarragon, and parsley or rosemary, thyme, and bay add
    according to taste
1 tsp salt
1 Tbs sugar
1 oz (30 g) vinegar
1½ oz (40 g) water

In a coffee mill grind the mustard seed very fine; then grind in the
herbs. Put the mustard-herb meal in a bowl, add vinegar, water,
sugar, and salt, and beat for at least 3 minutes with an electric
beater. The mustard will be good after at least 1 week; before
that it is too sharp.

Cheese in a Jar

1 branch rosemary
1 branch thyme
1 bay leaf
5 cloves garlic
10 fresh chili peppers
20 black olives
7 oz (200 g) goat cheese
2 C (½ L) olive oil

Cut cheese into cubes and arrange decoratively in a large jar
with the herbs, peppers, olives, and whole garlic cloves. Pour
olive oil over, cover the jar, and let stand in a dark place. After
4–5 days the cheese will have taken up the flavors of the herbs.
Serve as an appetizer or a snack on bread.

Salted Vegetables

1 bunch parsley
1 bunch celery with root and leaves
2 C (450 g) each of carrots, leek, and tomatoes
2 C (450 g) salt

Puree herbs and vegetables and add salt. Stir occasionally for 2
days. In tightly closed jars the mixture will keep for over a year. It
can be used as seasoning for soups and sauces.

Rosemary Wine

4 branches fresh rosemary
1 qt (1 L) semidry white wine

Wash rosemary and pat dry; place in the wine bottle. Store herbed wine in a cool place for two weeks, then strain and place in a decorative bottle. Use as an aperitif.

Peppermint Liqueur

15 stalks peppermint
1 qt (1 L) clear liqueur
2 C (½ L) water
17½ oz (500 g) sugar
grated peel of 1 lemon

Wash peppermint and coarsely chop. Add to a large jar, pour liqueur over it. Allow to steep in a warm place. After 2 weeks add lemon peel; 2 weeks later boil up sugar and water, cool and add to the strained herb-alcohol mixture. Allow to stand overnight, then pour into bottles and store in a cool place. The liqueur can be used after 3 months; the older it gets, the stronger its flavor.

Herbed Pork Loin

About 3½ oz (100 g) each of herbs: rosemary, thyme, and
   oregano
a pinch of sage
2 cloves garlic
1 pork loin

Rub pork loin with oil and salt and cover with herbs and finely minced garlic. Roast for 30 minutes per pound at 350°F (180°C)

Kitchen Herbs—Planting/Harvest Chart

A = annual plants
B = biennial plants

P = perennial plants
I–XII = months

Plant Name	Page	Annual, Perennial	Also as Pot Plant	Sowing/ Planting Time	Harvest Time	Useable Portions of Plant
Angelica	22	P	–	IX	V–X	leaves, roots
Anise	3	A	–	III–IV	VI–VII	seeds
Basil	4	A	X	V	XI–IX	leaves
Bay Tree	23	P	X	IV–V	VIII–X	leaves
Bee Balm	24	P	–	IV–V	VII–IX	leaves
Borage	5	A	X	IV	VII–VIII	leaves
Burnet	25	P	–	III	V–IX	leaves
Caraway	18	B	X	IV	VI–VIII	leaves, seeds
Celery	19	B	–	V	VII–IX	leaves, roots
Chervil	6	A	X	III–IV	V–VIII	leaves
Chili Pepper	7	A	X	V	IX–X	fruits
Chives	26	P	X	IV–V	I–XII	leaves
Coriander	8	A	–	IV	VIII–IX	seeds
Dill	9	A	X	IV	VI–X	leaves, seeds
Fennel	10	A	X	IV	V–VII	leaves, seeds

Garlic	11	A	X	III–IV	V–VIII	bulbs
Geraniums, fragrant	27	P	X	IV–V	I–XII	leaves
Hyssop	28	P	–	IV–V	VII	leaves
Juniper	29	P	X	IV–V	X	berries
Lemon Balm	30	P	X	IV–V	V–X	leaves
Lovage	31	P	X	IV	VI–IX	leaves
Marjoram, Sweet	17	A	X	V	V–X	leaves
Mustard	12	A	X	IV	VII–X	leaves, seeds
Mugwort	32	P	–	IV–V	VI–IX	leaves
Nasturtium	13	A	X	V	VII–X	leaves, flowers
Oregano	33	P	X	IV–V	VI–XI	leaves, flowers
Parsley	20	B	X	V	VII–IX	leaves
Pepper-grass	14	A	X	III–IV	IV–XI	leaves
Peppermint	34	P	X	V	VII–IX	leaves
Purslane	15	A	X	V	VI	leaves
Rosemary	35	P	X	IV–V	V–XI	leaves
Sage	36	P	X	IV–V	V–XI	leaves
Scurvy Grass	21	B	X	III	V–XII	leaves
Sorrel	37	P	X	V	VI–VIII	young leaves

Continued on next page

A = annual plants   P = perennial plants
B = biennial plants   I–XII = months

Plant Name	Page	Annual, Perennial	Also as Pot Plant	Sowing/ Planting Time	Harvest Time	Useable Portions of Plant
Southern-wood	38	P	X	IV–V	VII–IX	leaves
Summer Savory	16	A	X	IV	VI–VIII	leaves
Tarragon	39	P	X	IV	VII–IX	leaves
Thyme	40	P	X	IV–V	V–X	leaves
Watercress	41	P	X	IV–V	VI–XII	leaves
Winter Savory	42	P	X	III–IV	VI–VII	leaves

Herbs Index

Allium
 sativum, 11
 schoenoprasum, 26
Anethum graveolens, 9
Angelica, 22
Angelica
 archangelica, 22
Anise, 3
Annual Marjoram, 17
Anthriscus
 cerefolium, 6
Apium graveolens, 19
Archangel, 22
Artemisia
 abrotanum, 38
 dracunculus, 39
 vulgaris, 32

Basil, 4
Bay Tree, 23
Bee Balm, 24, 30
B. nigra, 12
Borage, 5
Borago officinalis, 5
Brassica hirta, 12
Burnet, 25

Calamint, 42
Capsicum annuum, 7
Caraway, 18
Carum carvi, 18
Celery, 19
Chervil, 6
Chili Pepper, 7
Chinese Parsley, 8
Chives, 26
Cochlearia
 officinalis, 21
Common Balm, 30
Common Sage, 36
Coriander, 8
Coriandrum
 sativum, 8

Dill, 9

Estragon, 39

Felon Herb, 32
Fennel, 10
Foeniculum vulgare, 10
Fragrant Geranium, 27

Garden Burnet, 25
Garden Sage, 36
Garlic, 11

Hyssop, 28
Hyssopus
 officinalis, 28

Indian Cress, 13

Juniper, 29
Juniperus
 communis, 29

Lauris nobilis, 23
Lemon Balm, 30
Lemon-scented
 Geranium, 27
Lepidum sativum, 14
Levisticum
 officinale, 31
Lovage, 31

Melissa officinalis, 30
Mentha piperita, 34
Monarda, 24
Monarda didyma, 24
Mugwort, 32
Mustard, 12

Nasturtium, 13
Nasturtium
 officinale, 41

Ocimum basilicum, 4
Old Man, 38
Oregano, 33
Origano, 33
Origanum
 majorana, 17
 vulgare, 33
Origany, 33
Oswego Tea, 24

Parsley, 20
Pelargonium
 graveolens/citrosum/
 tomentosum, 27
Peppergrass, 14
Peppermint, 34
Peppermint
 Geranium, 27

Pepperwort, 14
Petroselinum
 crispum, 20
Pimpinella anisum, 3
Portulaca oleracea, 15
Pot Marjoram, 33
Purslane, 15
Pusley, 15

Rose Geranium, 27
Rosemary, 35
Rosmarinus
 officinalis, 35
Rumex acetosa, 37

Sage, 36
Salad chervil, 6
Salvia officinalis, 36
Sanguisorba minor, 25
Satureja
 hortensis, 16
 montana, 42
Scurvy Grass, 21
Sorrel, 37
Sour Dock, 37
Southernwood, 38
Spoonwort, 21
Summer Savory, 16
Sweet Balm, 30
Sweet Marjoram, 17

Tall Nasturtium, 13
Tarragon, 39
Thyme, 40
Thymus vulgaris, 40
Tonguegrass, 14
Tropaeolum majus, 13

Watercress, 41
Wild Marjoram, 33
Wild Parsnip, 22
Winter Savory, 42

English translation © Copyright 1991 by Barron's Educational Series, Inc.

© Copyright 1988 by Gräfe and Unzer GmbH, Munich, West Germany
The title of the German book is *Küchen Kräuter*

Translated from the German by Elizabeth D. Crawford.

All rights reserved.
No part of this book may be reproduced in any form, by photostat, microfilm, xerography, or any other means, or incorporated into any information retrieval system, electronic or mechanical, without the written permission of the copyright owner.

All inquiries should be addressed to:
Barron's Educational Series, Inc.
250 Wireless Boulevard
Hauppauge, New York 11788

Library of Congress Catalog Card No. 90-20157

International Standard Book No. 0-8120-4453-3

Library of Congress Cataloging-in-Publication Data

Recht, Christine.
  [Küchen Kräuter. English]
  Herbs. / by Christine Recht; translated by Elizabeth D. Crawford.
    p. cm. — (Barron's mini fact finders)
  Translation of: Küchen Kräuter.
  ISBN 0-8120-4453-3
  1. Herbs. 2. Herb gardening. 3. Cookery (Herbs) I. Title.
II. Series.
SB351.H5R4313 1991
635'.7—dc20
                                                                    90-20157
PRINTED IN HONG KONG   CIP
1234 4900 987654321

Photographs: Bellmann: 32; Burda: back cover; Eigstler: 42; Flora-Bild: 17; Photo-Center: 5, 12 top, 13, 38; Reinhard, 8, 10, 12 bottom, 20, 24, 28, 34, 35; Scherz, 7, 19 left, 29, 37, front cover; Schimmitat: 18; Schimmitat/Angerer: 3; Schrempp: 22, 25, 26, 31, 33, 36, 40; Silvestris/Wothe: 27; Teubner: 47, 57; Vonarburg: 6, 16, 30; Wetterwald: 23, 39, inside front cover (6); Wothe: 4, 9, 11, 14, 15, 19 right, 21.